Branding with Type

Branding with Type

Stefan Rögener
Albert-Jan Pool
Ursula Packhäuser

edited by E.M.Ginger
translated by
Stephanie Tripier

Adobe Press
Mountain View
California

Library of Congress Catalog No.: 95-80 299

ISBN 1 56830 248 7

10 9 8 7 6 5 4 3 2 First Printing: November 1995

*Printed in the United States of America. Published simultaneously
in Canada.*

*Published and distributed to the trade by Hayden Books, a division
of Macmillan Computer Publishing. For individual, retail, corporate, educational and government sales information, contact
Macmillan Computer Publishing, 201 W. 103rd Street, Indianapolis,
Indiana, 46290 USA, or call, 317-581-3500.*

*For information on the original German edition of this book,
entitled* Typen machen Marken Mächtig *contact AdFinder GmbH,
Poststrasse 3, D 20354 Hamburg, Germany
or call +49 (40) 37 35 15 or fax +49 (40) 36 77 98*

Type, layout, and color make up the equilateral triangle of brand identity.

Stefan Rögener
Type consultant, Germany

A professional typesetter for many years, Stefan Rögener is naturally interested in who is using which typefaces. In the late 1980s he began to analyse thousands of ad campaigns for their typographic content. The first results were staggering: "Helvetica, Futura, Times, and Garamond were used 90 percent of the time; give me a pistol!"

Type: Walbaum Buch

Preface

Illustration: John Miles, Banks & Miles, London.

Looking for the right type

Type is magical. It not only communicates
a word's information, but it conveys a
subliminal message in the letter shapes
themselves. That civilizations created reli-
gious icons from letters and symbols is
not without foundation. Good typography
significantly increases the amount of attention a message receives: The right typeface
is the basis of strong communication.

Type alone cannot sustain a brand name
or a corporate identity, but a brand with
the wrong typeface will flounder helplessly
trying to define itself. Type, layout, and
color make up the equilateral triangle of
brand identity. Like everything else in life,
to be successful with type you have to first
choose the right one, and then use it well.

There is no foolproof recipe for selecting
the right type for each and every purpose.
Choosing the right type requires experience, intuition, and creativity. Which type
best suits the headline, subhead, and copy
of an ad, which for packaging design, which
for technical products, and which for food
– in-depth research is necessary before an
informed decision can be made. The final
arbiter is a matter of taste.

This book looks at a few ways to unravel
the mysteries of type, while it sets up a
series of guidelines for the intelligent choice
of the right one.

Stefan Rögener

There are numerous typographic rules. The most important is: Do not ever do it the way someone else does.

Kurt Schwitters (1887 – 1948)
Painter and writer, Germany

Kurt Schwitters integrated his dadaist poetry and typography into collages he called "Merzkunst." For him, text and typography were inseparable.

Type: Berthold Block

**Branding
with type**

More success with the "secret weapon" type

Branding with type

There are still art directors who use creative typography to give power to brand identities in the marketplace. Powerful type! It doesn't have to be a proprietary design, which is affordable only by large firms. For example, Mercedes has been using Corporate ASE for its identity since 1990. Art director Karl Gerstner chose Berthold Bodoni for IBM's international markets fourteen years ago. And Marlboro, the world's bestselling cigarette, has been riding successfully on Neo Contact for twenty years. How do these extraordinary brand successes happen? What role does the type play, and what does an audience see when it looks at type?

Computer

Puzzle:
Look carefully at the word "computer." Something is not quite right. Do you have a strange feeling about it? Find out what is wrong.

Answer:
The word "computer" is set in the "Marlboro typeface" Neo Contact. Your head reads "computer," but your intuition says "Marlboro." This is an example of how type influences the subconscious.

The subconscious reacts in a large variety of ways to even the most minimal stimuli. Sensory impressions are connected to symbols – that is to say, coded – and stored in the subconscious as experience. Symbols can activate experiences at any given time and bring them forward to the conscious level.

The most widely used symbols are letters. Type, in its incredible diversity of form, carries coded information that is completely independent of the content of the transmitted message. Before a single word is consciously read, the subconscious re-

WAS WIR AM HÄNDLER SPAREN SIE AM COMPUTER.

Drei Jahre mit Be- währung!

Campaign: Dell Computer; Type: Futura extra bold

Witty text, striking layout – but the Marlboro success story will never happen here. The uniqueness value of this typeface is zero! One shouldn't save in the wrong place – choosing a typeface.

Campaign: Rank Xerox; Type: Times Roman

The clean design helps distinguish this ad from the rest of the daily fare. But the opportunity to link a brand with an original typeface was missed. Even after three years, this typography doesn't work as an image builder.

sponds to the physical characteristics of the type – weight, curves, serifs, descenders, rhythm. The complete package – for example, perfume xyz's brand name – is grasped as a symbol and stored together with associated information. The information, which could be the perfume's scent or a nice experience one had in connection with it, is immediately brought to mind when looking at the "symbol."

You are driving on a clear, straight road.

A lorry pulls out from a side road directly in front of you.

You can't stop.

You can't avoid it.

You hit it.

What happens in the next ⅓₀th of a second?

De oorlog is voorbij.

De oorlog is voorbij. De maar is genullen. Apple introduceert de Power Macintosh™. Krachtiger dan een PC, nog gebruikersvriendelijker dan een Macintosh, en meer compatibel dan beide. Hij is uitgerust met een PowerPC™ chip, een nieuwe processor die nog krachtiger is, nog sneller werkt, en toepassingen mogelijk maakt die u nu tot onderelkaar voren. In zowel een Macintosh, MS-DOS als Windows omgeving.

1 2

4 5

Auf den nächsten Seiten sehen Sie ein neues Glück.

A timeless land. Where horses still run free. Where some men do what others only dream about.

A logo or text image is not only recognized on a conscious level, but is available for future reference when we recall the experience. Typography influences the subconscious so strongly that conditioning the observer with type is not only possible but definitely happens – whether we want it to or not. The designer can direct this process consciously to the advantage of the brand's identity. This is a singular opportunity to link an advertising message to a typeface that deciphers *only this* message, and so with every viewing, summons *only this* message.

Wie Sie Qualität blau auf weiß erkennen können: Aral Super reinigt und schützt vor Korrosion. Damit Ihr Motor nicht mehr verbraucht, als er braucht.

Branding with type

3

6

Mit unserem Attraktiv-Tarif* können Sie ihr ein Häuschen auf Erden versprechen.

On the other hand, setting a message in Helvetica or Times forces a brand to share its space in the audience's subconscious with thousands of other brands. There is no possibility of recognition at this level: Helvetica is already subconsciously coded as "indifferent appeal, boring, forgettable." The advertising designer is left to rely on (hoped for) unique copy or (hoped for) creative illustration to deliver the product's message. This leaves the ad copy and illustration to do what should have been the business of the typography.

IBM PS/1.
Fem minutter
-og du er i gang

Diese Woche
von IBM:
In 80 Sekunden
um die Welt.

Campaign: IBM; Type: Berthold Bodoni-Antiqua; Countries: Denmark, Germany

The right combination, however, of product, ad pitch, and illustration makes it possible to grab the last 10 percent of attention with the typeface. The subconscious knows if a typeface is masculine, and which script faces signal individuality, wildness, or tenderness. It knows that type with fanciful loops means luxury and that finely made letters reflect the delicate form of a woman. It knows that rough headlines slam into the consciousness and that whimsical letter designs stimulate playfulness. An experienced typographer also knows these things – he or she will design and

Nivea is a mega brand that has achieved international identity success with the consistent use of their corporate typeface – an accomplishment that most competitors only dream about.

Their success is not a coincidence, nor is it out of the reach of market strategists. Type is not everything for success in the international marketplace, but without it, an ad campaign is nothing.

create codes for feelings, allowing easy access to that unique place in the sub-conscious.

All major brand successes were created this way. Anyone who can handle type creatively and intelligently can be just as successful.

Typography is like
cooking or lovemaking
in that there is
basically little that
is new …
Typography is the art
of the fine touch:
too little and too
gentle takes away
from mastery just as
too much and too
rough does.

Kurt Weidemann
Designer, consultant, Germany

*Kurt Weidemann is the designer of
ITC Weidemann, and is a typographic
consultant to Daimler Benz, for which
he developed the typeface trilogy
Corporate A·S·E.*

Type: Corporate A

**How to
identify type**

The art of type classification

Designers should be able to choose and decide about type as confidently as they do color. Very few designers would like to be restricted to just using red, green, and blue. We take the time to make red into brick red, green into apple green, and blue into sky blue. It's fun and the 16 million avail-able colors offer unlimited design possibilities.

Old Style roman

    Choosing type presents the same oppor-tunities, and there are innumerable sources from which we can draw freely. Like colors, typefaces differ by rather small details: letter widths, stem widths, the shapes of curves, and the proportions of serifs.

Transitional roman

Times Garamond	Helvetica Futura
roman types	*sans serif types*

Modern roman

The difficulty of choice

It's not easy. There are thousands of avail-able typefaces and it is a time-consuming task to find the ideal one for every project. And type vendors do not make it any easier. Type catalogs are usually indexed alphabetically, or by manufacturer, not by type style, which would be the logical way to do it. Alphabetical entries are helpful only to those who want to know where to get a particular typeface. Color books, for instance, have all the reds together – colors are not listed under specific names such as Bordeaux red, blue, and brown because they all happen to begin with B. Those who do not know the names of all the type-faces are in the unfortunate situation of having to spend many hours poring over type catalogs.

Textura

Fraktur

Fortunately, even if we don't know exactly what we are looking for, we do know the general direction in which to look. Roman or sans serif is the first question asked about type, and this chapter will clear up that basic issue. Take a look at Garamond, Times, Helvetica, and Futura.

The most prominent features:
Serifs and contrast

Just as colors are sorted by primary colors, typefaces can be classified by primary shapes. Typefaces are divided into two main categories: roman (seriffed) and sans serif. (The term "roman" is also used to describe letters that are upright, i.e., roman and italic.) At first glance, the difference is whether the type has serifs or not.

Removing the serifs from Garamond, however, does not give us Univers. Likewise, we don't get Garamond if we give Univers serifs, we get something that looks like Serifa.

Roman

Garamond
roman

Roman?

Univers "with" (Serifa)
slab serif linear

Sans Serif?

Garamond "without"
sans serif roman

Sans Serif

Univers
sans serif linear

This brings us to the second difference, which is contrast. In type design this is the comparative difference between thick and thin letter strokes. All classification systems refer to roman and sans serif. The example shows that we can also distinguish between typefaces with high contrast and low contrast. Linear typefaces with serifs, such as Serifa, are called slab serif. A sans serif roman is often referred to as a "modified" or "humanist" sans serif.

typeface classification

Roman & *Italic*

Adobe Garamond
Old Style

Roman & *Italic*

Adobe Caslon
Transitional

Roman & *Italic*

Berthold Bodoni
Modern

Roman & *Italic*

Serifa
slab serif linear

Roman & *Italic*

Helvetica
sans serif linear

Roman & *Italic*

Optima
sans serif roman

Roman & **Roman**

Alcuin, Dom Casual
Script

Italic & Italic

ITC Zapf Chancery, English Script
Script
(broad nib, pointed nib)

Textura & Fraktur

Old English Text, Walbaum Fraktur
Blackletter

Different contrast varieties

If we take our "Garamond sans serif" and
thicken the thin strokes, a typeface similar
to Syntax or Gill Sans appears. The same
procedure could result in PMN Caecilia
from Garamond. If we make the horizontal
strokes thinner, Univers becomes similar to
Optima, and Serifa looks like Bodoni. This
procedure would not turn Garamond into
a Univers. Why not?

*slab serif
linear*

Hamburger

Garamond
Old Style roman

Hamburger

Garamond "without"
sans serif roman

Hamburger

Gill "with" (PMN Caecilia)
Old Style slab serif

Hamburger

Gill Sans
Old Style sans serif

Hamburger

Bodoni
Modern roman

Hamburger

Bodoni "without"
sans serif roman

Hamburger

Univers "with" (Serifa)
Modern slab serif

Hamburger

Univers
Modern sans serif

*heavy serif
Old Style*

*heavy serif
Transitional*

*heavy serif
Modern*

The two different kinds of contrast originated from the handwriting from which
the latin alphabet was developed. The contrast of Old Style letterforms is derived
from scripts that were written with a
broad-nibbed pen, while Modern typefaces
show the traces of a flexible-nibbed pen.
The illustration above shows that the traditions of Old Style and Modern design have
a distinct impact on sans serif and slab
serif types.

Special types for exceptional legibility

In the 1930s Mergenthaler Linotype
designed five typefaces specifically for
newspaper settings. Each of the types in
the "Legibility Group" has emphasized

serifs and generous counterforms (the white space inside letters).

These typefaces were designed to be legible under the poorest printing conditions. They are still quite useful for settings on colored, screened, or patterned backgrounds. The legibility typefaces are classified as Modern, but types with similar legibility standards have also been developed in Old Style and Transitional classes.

Type mixes and type bastardizations

The second parallel to color is that two contrast varieties can clash with each other typographically – these combinations will frequently expose typographic weaknesses. It is sometimes said that one should not mix roman and sans serif typefaces, which is not necessarily so. Combining a light Bodoni with a bold Helvetica is a safe bet because of their similar contrasts, but putting together a Bodoni and Garamond in a similar size and weight might be thought radical. The end result is what counts, and a mix of type styles can be as wrong or right as a color mixture. It works or it doesn't, depending on the context in which it is used.

Helvetica

Helvetica headline contrasted with Bodoni copy.

Helvetica

The headline looks better in a bolder Helvetica, the proportions are more distinct.

Bodoni

It might be adventurous to set a Bodoni headline over Garamond copy. It is not especially eye-catching.

Bodoni

Creating a conspicuous contrast sometimes stimulates interest.

Legibility

Excelsior, designed in 1931, is a typeface from the Mergenthaler Linotype "Legibility Group" (Ionic, Excelsior, Opticon, Paragon, Corona)

Legibility

With the release of LinoLetter in 1993, Linotype ensured the next generation of legibility types.

Hamburger	Hamburger	Hamburger
Berthold Garamond *Old Style roman*	Adobe Caslon *Transitional roman*	Berthold Bodoni *Modern roman*
Hamburger	Hamburger	Hamburger
Swift *heavy serif Old Style*	ITC Cushing *heavy serif Transitional*	Melior *heavy serif Modern*
Hamburger	Hamburger	Hamburger
PMN Caecilia *Old Style slab serif*	Rockwell *Transitional slab serif*	Serifa *Modern slab serif*

With so many new typeface variations, type classifications have almost become obsolete. However, you can still count on Bodoni and Garamond falling into the right classification slots. But Gill Sans and Helvetica – very different from each other – are often classified the same; and so it is for PMN Caecilia and Serifa.

The Transitional roman historically represents the shift from Old Style to Modern. These Transitional faces also exist between slab serif typefaces PMN Caecilia and Serifa and the heavy serif typefaces Swift and Melior (Page 25).

Optima

Latienne

Latin Wide

Hamburg

Optima
sans serif roman

Hamburg

Latienne
latin roman

Hamburg

Latin Wide
latin roman

Hamburg

Rotis Serif

Hamburg

Rotis Semi Serif

Hamburg

Rotis Semi Sans

Hamburg

Rotis Sans Serif

Old Style italic

Modern italic

heavy serif italic

An interesting variation is the sans serif roman. Officially a sans serif, many of these typefaces have small, quasi-suggestive serifs that seem to bud out of the main letter strokes, creating a combination of roman and sans serif. The opposite of this is the so-called "latin" with its large, triangular serifs. The Latienne typeface has both features.

Lastly, take note of the unusual Rotis family, which has both a Semi Serif and a Semi Sans.

Geometry

Typeface design is sometimes the result of a break from historical traditions. In the fifteenth century, the Italians, for example, introduced their comparatively light roman types in response to the rather blackish textura and fraktur types of Western Europe. Firmin Didot and Giambattista Bodoni broke with the Old Style tradition when they introduced the Modern style.

The Bauhaus movement in the 1920s experimented with the popular sans serif faces introduced in the nineteenth century – the most famous design rendition of this "new kind of roman typeface" is Paul Renner's Futura. Next is ITC Bauhaus, a revival of Herbert Bayer's experiments with letter shapes. Today, Futura looks stiff and conservative, but the geometrics continue to evolve and now have their own, almost independent, style direction. Examples are Neville Brody's typefaces and those of his innumerable followers.

Italics

An entirely new type vista opens up when we consider the italic counterparts of the typefaces we have looked at. Many sans serif and slab serif typefaces (for example, Helvetica and Serifa) have italic companions that are different only in angle. Most typefaces, however, have "true italics" – separate designs that are generally more energetic than their roman counterparts.

Recognizing faces

The type classifications discussed above give a basic understanding of how type is grouped, and where many of the thousands of typefaces fit in.

Like human siblings or twins, the differences among typefaces are often very subtle. Typefaces, too, have similar faces, but whoever loves them will recognize them!

How to identify type

Futura

1928 Futura is released.
For the first time the clear, simple shapes of the Bauhaus are given to the roman typeface.

ITC Avant Garde

In 1970, ITC
(International Type Corporation)
releases its first typeface,
ITC Avant Garde Gothic.

ITC Bauhaus

Five years later Ed Benguiat
and Vic Caruso transform
Herbert Bayer's letter experiments
into ITC Bauhaus.

Avenir

In 1988 Linotype commissions type designer Adrian Frutiger to develop the geometric Avenir.

Industria & Insignia

Neville Brody's letterforms
have become a familiar style
since 1990.

Before using a beautiful word, one has to give it the right context.

Joseph Joubert (1754 – 1824)
Moralist, France

Type: DTL Fleischmann

Typeface profiles

How type works

Smart type choices enhance the advertising message. This is a given, but how do type-faces look on their own?

Certain typefaces summon direct responses because we constantly see them used for specific products. We would therefore associate Times with scientific material rather than baby food, Optima with cosmetics rather than gasoline, and Corporate ASE with cars rather than beverages.

ITC Legacy Serif
static

ITC Legacy Serif
dynamic

Only Type Can Make Words Beautiful

Please judge the above type on the qualities below.
Mark the degree of the mentioned quality you think the type has.

very playful	4	3	2	1	0	not playful at all
very extravagant	4	3	2	1	0	not extravagant at all
very sporty	4	3	2	1	0	not sporty at all
very modern	4	3	2	1	0	not modern at all

Univers
masculine

Optima
feminine

Such correlations are not just the result of habit. Even obscure typefaces elicit moods in the observer. The type designer gives his or her creation its shape, which is the language that speaks to the senses. From a scientific standpoint we don't know much about the effects of typography, as compared to color, for example. It is certain, though, that readers have similar feelings about certain typefaces. The selection of a typeface for an advertising message, therefore, is more than a subjective exercise, and it is certainly not arbitrary or inconsequential.

At this point in time theoretical research results are not one of a designer's tools. The selection of type depends on many factors, as you will see in the chapter "How to find the right typeface."

We still must rely on intuition and instinct. A good way to develop this sixth sense for type is to set up polarity profiles. Polarity profiles are reliable tools for analyzing the effects of type. They can be used, for example, to assess several different ad designs, or for market research that quantifies and statistically evaluates the reactions of a target group to a headline set in several different typefaces.

Using selected examples, we want to find out something about the expectation of typefaces. Contrary examples are always set up opposite one another.

Static or dynamic

How and where a typeface appears determines the impression it makes. Lower case letters appear dynamic and full of life next to capitals, but seem static when compared to italics.

CAPITALS	lower case
roman	*italic*
SMALL CAPS	**bold**
ITC Legacy Serif	
formal	*informal*
static	*dynamic*

Rugged or elegant

One might assume that serifs are the most important factors for determining a typeface's impact, but this is not necessarily so. Frequently the question is: Does a typeface appear more masculine or more feminine, more rugged or more elegant? These reactions are not determined by the serifs as much as by the degree of contrast between letter strokes.

H

Serifa
rugged

U

ITC Zapf
International
elegant

B

ITC Berkeley
Old Style
extravagant

C

ITC Franklin Gothic
economical

Linear	Roman
Univers	Optima
Linear	Roman
Serifa	ITC Zapf International
masculine *rugged*	*feminine* *elegant*

ITC Zapf Chancery
complex

Extravagant or economical

Typefaces with slightly higher contrast, pronounced serifs, and ornamental features convey impressions such as "expensive" and "special" because of their complex structure. Comparatively, typefaces with low contrast seem very plain.

ITC Studio Script
plain

Roman	Linear
ITC Berkeley Old Style	ITC Franklin Gothic
Calligraphy	**Script**
ITC Zapf Chancery	Dom Casual
Calligraphy	*Script*
English Script	ITC Studio Script
formal *extravagant* *complex*	*informal* *economical* *plain*

Avenir
technical

n

Today Sans Serif
natural

Technical or natural

Geometric shapes bring technical elements into the picture. The more dynamic shapes of Today Sans Serif and URW Alcuin are their counterpoints.

Severe or gentle

Even attributes like severe and gentle can be expressed with the right typeface. Typefaces with fine, sharp serifs and geometric shapes appear more severe, while those with rounded edges or strokes seem more

Geometric   Old Style

Avenir   Today Sans Serif

Geometric   Old Style

Futura   URW Alcuin

formal   *informal*
technical   *natural*

ITC Galliard
angular

Cooper Black
curved

gentle. Using the corresponding typeface reinforces the headline message.

Traditional or trendy

Originally created out of necessity, stencils are now independent typefaces, having become their own typographical style. The traditional stencil represents temporary sale items, reminding us of the hand-lettering on boxes and bags and on signs in markets. New eye-catching variations based on sans serif and slab serif styles have enlarged white slashes inside the letters.

ITC Goudy Sans
severe

ITC Highlander
gentle

Hamburg   **Hamburg**

ITC Galliard   Cooper Black

Hamburg   **Hamburg**

ITC Goudy Sans   ITC Highlander

Hamburg   **Hamburg**

ITC Avant Garde Gothic   Letraset Frankfurter

angular   *curved*
hard   *soft*
severe   *gentle*

Hamburg
Bernhard Antique

HAMBURG
Stencil

Hamburg
Berliner Grotesk

HAMBURG
Glaser Stencil

Hamburg
Berthold Block

Hamburg
URW City Stencil

romantic
dated
traditional

practical
fresh
trendy

Berliner Grotesk
dated

Glaser Stencil
fresh

Romantic or practical

Typefaces with irregular contours can make headlines appear "old-fashioned." They convey time-honored traditions and nostalgia – they are therefore frequently called "Antique." Bolder and lower contrast types appear more practical.

Sensitive or coarse

The most noticeable differences in typefaces are their weights. While light types appear fine, reserved, and subtle, bold typefaces signal the contrary: strong, loud, and conspicuous, they force themselves into your field of vision. In between are the "normal" typefaces that appear neutral, prudent, and balanced.

Berthold Block
traditional

URW City Stencil
trendy

Hamburg
Optima

Hamburg
Berthold Baskerville Book

Hamburg
ITC Souvenir

Hamburg
Today Sans Serif

Hamburg
Frutiger

Hamburg
Helvetica

reserved
subtle

balanced
neutral

loud
economical

Danish	„G"			*Polish*	„G" »G«		
Dutch	„G" 'G' «G»			*Portuguese*	«G» "G"	*	
Czech	„G" »G«			*Rumanian*	„G"		
English	"G" 'G'			*Russian*	«G» „G"		
Finnish	"G" »G»			*Swedish*	"G" »G»		
French	« G »	one-quarter em space between		*Swiss*	„G" «G»		
	"G"	*		*Serbocroatian*	»G« „G"	*	
German	„G" »G«			*Slavonic*	„G" «G»		
Hungarian	„G" „G"			*Slovakian*	„G" »G«		
Italian	« G »	one-eighth em space between		*Spanish*	"G"		
Norwegian	«G» „G"	*		*Turkish*	«G» "G"		

*Quotation marks
and the "little difference"*

What's the difference between Danes, Germans, Poles, and Hungarians and the English, Americans, French, and Swedes? Everyone can think of something – language, food, currency, manners … What is less well known is that every language, and country, has its own way of using quotation marks.

It is probably only just a matter of time, however, before this last bastion of charming national custom gets a universal Euro-norm from Brussels! Until then we can only say "Vive la différence!"

Germans use the little saying "99 bottom – 66 top" to remind themselves of the correct order. For the alternate "duck's feet" they use "double pointer right and left pointing." The opposite, "double pointer left and right pointing" brings to mind the expansive southern gestures of the French and Italians, seeming to say "Look out, here I come!" The reader almost loses context if there are one-eighth or one-quarter em spaces in between.

* For French, Portuguese, and Serbocroatian, the form listed on the right is generally used for headlines.

the hardest thing to see is what is in front of your eyes.

Johann Wolfgang von Goethe (1749 – 1826)
Poet, Germany

Calligraphy by Jovica Veljović, designer of
ITC Veljovic, ITC Esprit, ITC Gamma, and Ex Ponto.

**How to find the
right typeface**

Criteria for choosing a typeface

How to find the right typeface

How do you find the right type for a brand, an ad campaign, a corporate identity, a catalog, or a packaging design? To be perfectly honest, there is no "formula." Nevertheless, designers should not rely only on intuition, and they especially should not settle for established successes because of convenience or insecurity. This chapter gives ideas and pointers for a systematic, yet creative, approach to finding the right type.

ITC New Baskerville
capital

The right typeface should fit the product while simultaneously visualizing the specific message, presenting the advertiser's image, and speaking directly to the target audience.

Adobe Caslon
lower case

Five key questions for success

1. Did it take my breath away the first time I saw it?
2. Do I wish I had thought it up myself?
3. Is it unforgettable?
4. Does it fit seamlessly into the advertising strategy of the company?
5. Will it still be good in thirty years?

In his book Ogilvy on Advertising, *the author wants the reader to ask him/herself five questions to judge the effectiveness of an ad. Beginning a design project with these questions in mind is a good way to start.*

Market research

Antique Olive
oblique

Industria
extra condensed

Latin Wide
extended

The basis of any well-founded decision on type is market observation and, if necessary, in-depth research. Look at the competition's ads, study design magazines and type catalogs.

The following questions should be answered:
– Which typeface(s) has been used (this country, other countries) up until now for the product?
– Which typefaces were and are used for the competitor's products?
– Which typeface is used by the market leader?
– Is there a type family specifically attached to this product group?

ITC Galliard
italic

Vendôme
condensed

ITC Berkeley
bold

If you don't have the appropriate material at hand or do not have the time to do the research yourself, you can contract the services of a professional type consultant.

Do not copy the market leader

This is the bottom line: Do not be satisfied too quickly. Using the typeface of the market leader does not ensure success. This actually only increases the degree of recognition for the market leader. However, under certain circumstances it can be useful to select a type with similar characteristics.

In each case, ask yourself: Are there any new typefaces that might give the message new expression? New can also mean new to this product group.

Determine the characteristics of the typeface

The next step is to define the characteristics of your ideal typeface with a polarity profile. You might choose pairs with opposite characteristics, such as businesslike – playful or classic – avant garde and then judge if and to what extent these characteristics apply to the ideal typeface.

Polarity profiles can also help determine the most important characteristics of the product itself and of the target group(s). The criteria are usually very product specific, but some generalizations apply everywhere.

Type weights

An advertising design seldom gets along with only one typeface in one size. So you have to decide: Can everything be done with only one type weight? (Note: not every text typeface is suitable for headline use.) Can I get along with just one type family? Does it have all the styles and weights I need (for example, italics, bold, etc.)? How do they differ? Do I have to choose another typeface to get a particular weight?

*Opposing pairs
for polarity profiles*

young – old
radical – conservative
low budget – high budget
new – old, reliable
sporty – intellectual
plain – luxurious
short lived – long lasting
leisurely – businesslike
modern – old-fashioned
masculine – feminine
proven – theoretical
poetic – technical

*Characteristics of products,
brands, target groups, and typefaces.
The list is endless.*

DTL Fleischmann
ligatures

ITC Cerigo
swashes

ITC Tiepolo
small caps

ITC Golden Type
old style figures

Goudy Handtooled
initial

Princetown
initial

Measures of style

Style definitions for type can also be useful
for visualizing special characteristics of
the product. See if there is agreement with
certain stylistic features of the product.
Does the product have a relationship to
a certain art historical period, to a country,
a cultural trend, or special area of life?

Thunderbird
Wild West

Contrasts

Interesting design contrasts can be evoked
by using very different typefaces (type
mixing). Decide if these contrasts suit the
product.

Arnold Böcklin
Art Nouveau

When working with various type weights,
widths, and styles (for example, extra black,
extended, italics) it is best to stay with one
family. Type designers have created the
different variations in many type families
so that type-mixes appear to be "from
the same mold." Stylistic *faux pas* are therefore impossible.

Sinaloa
Art Deco

Several of these extended type families
contain some surprises: The "Stones" come
not only in Sans and Serif but also Informal, and the new FF Thesis has a separate
weight called "The Mix." Also remarkable
in this context is Bordeaux. It is not an
especially large family, but it unites the
often-difficult-to-combine longhand script
with roman in one family.

Binner
Roaring Twenties

Futura
Bauhaus

Legibility

Legibility plays an important role in de-
ciding the type size and the intended venue
for publication. Are you looking for a pure
logotype, or a headline typeface for a
poster? Is the most important issue the
readability of small type in a catalog or
copy displayed on a monitor? There are
typefaces more or less appropriate for
every case.

DIN Mittelschrift
Conformist Fifties

Even the smallest sizes of type should be
legible. Newspaper printing and photogra-
vure are the worst-case scenarios when
it comes to unpredictable printing results.

Davida
Flower Power

Background colors, screens, or pictures can also inhibit type clarity. Compensate for these situations with a stronger typeface or a bolder weight, lighten up the background, put an outline around the type, or drop out the background entirely.

Headlines

When it comes to setting headlines there is practically no rule without an exception. Anything that can maintain the balance between conspicuousness and legibility is acceptable. There is, however, one hard and fast rule: Don't set long headlines in all caps. They are 30 percent more difficult to read, and when faced with more than twenty words set in all caps, most readers will not even attempt to read them.

Where do I find the right type?

The actual typeface choice can be made with the help of type specimen books (see bibliography). Buy new books – an up-to-date library is a good investment.

The other possibility is the software of the type manufacturer. Type CDs, type installation and management programs are more than just technical aids. Several companies have type browsers which allow users to look at and compare typefaces, and print out samples.

There are large quality differences even among typefaces. Bad type creates a bad image! Use only licensed original typefaces and avoid pirated copies.

Styles of typesetting

After finding the right typeface, make sure that weight, contrast, letter and word spacing, and line feed are well-balanced; this also affects the overall effectiveness of the design.

Compare the work of a typographer with that of a photographer. The photographer doesn't just take a picture. He or she conceptualizes, styles, lights. After

ITC Stone

Hamburgefonts
Hamburgefonts
Stone Sans medium & italic

Hamburgefonts
Hamburgefonts
Stone Serif medium & italic

Hamburgefonts
Hamburgefonts
Stone Informal medium & italic

FF Thesis

Hamburgefonts
Hamburgefonts
The Sans bold & italic

Hamburgefonts
Hamburgefonts
The Mix bold & italic

Hamburgefonts
Hamburgefonts
The Serif bold & italic

Letraset Bordeaux

Hamburgefonts
Bordeaux regular

Hamburgefonts
Bordeaux italic

Hamburgefonts
Bordeaux Script

the session the pictures are processed,
re-touched, colors are separated, and then
the photograph is integrated into the layout. Typography also requires many steps.
Experiment with several styles of your

Lithos
Cooper Black

Ice Age
ITC Legacy Serif

Univers
Antique Olive Nord

Baker Signet
Albertus

URW Oklahoma
ITC Eras

Balloon
ITC Beesknees

chosen typeface to make sure the letters
don't disintegrate, drown, or lose sharpness
or depth.

Effects

Even the dot over an i can make a typographical difference. Less is more, so caution must be exercised. Surely the goal
is missed if typographic effects push the
message into the background.

The presentation

The typeface choice should be on the list
of important design elements presented to
the client – it should not be treated as an
afterthought.

Explain how you decided to suggest this or that typeface. Make it clear that the decision was not arbitrary, and explain your reasoning and research in an understandable way.

Ways to find a typeface

The easy way

- The client determines the typeface
- I use my favorite typeface
- I use a standard typeface, that way nothing can go wrong
- I use a system typeface from the Mac or PC
- I use the typeface of a successful competitor
- I don't waste any time on extra research
- I stay with the client's current campaign
- I choose a typeface the client will immediately like
- I leave the decision to my assistant

The right way

- I'm lucky – the client has a good corporate typeface
- I look for the most fitting typeface
- I look for an unusual typeface that hasn't been used yet
- I study the latest type specimen books and font offers
- I do a product and type analysis and avoid the competitor's typeface
- I search for inspiration in domestic and foreign magazines
- I compare several ad campaigns
- I try to persuade the client to accept my type decision
- I have an exclusive typeface designed

Create type consciousness!

The client should realize that the type decision is an important part of product politics and that the success of the advertising campaign is directly influenced by the correct typeface choice.

This common-sense approach is advantageous when the decision to award a contract is imminent.

Oxen cannot convey
as much as beauty.

English proverb

Type can express qualities that may seem contrary at first glance. A fine example of this is PMN Caecilia, which has sturdy slab serifs that are carefully balanced with elegant curves.

Type: PMN Caecilia

**Put the pedal
to the metal**

International car advertising

Put the pedal to the metal

There isn't a product that requires consumer brand identification as much as cars. Special attention should be given to clearly defining the identity of the product – then informed, creative typography can be put into place. What types have been successful in car advertising? We found some answers by looking at car advertising in Germany, Great Britain, and the United States for the years 1990 to 1995.

The results: type variety

In total, 86 different typefaces were used in the examined ads. This initially looks encouraging and seems to refute the general opinion that six typefaces will work for everything that needs to be set.

But these figures are deceptive: In reality, only six or seven typefaces were used for 60 percent of the headlines, subheads, and copy in Germany. In England about twice as many typefaces are used for 60 percent of occurrences, and in the United States there are at least nine different typefaces.

The research method

Example 1: Volkswagen Ad in Germany 1990
Headline Futura, Subhead Futura, Copy Times:
3 occurrences, 2 points to Futura, 1 point to Times.

Example 2: BMW Ad in USA 1994
Headline Helvetica, no Subhead, Copy Garamond:
2 occurrences, 1 point to Helvetica, 1 point to Garamond.

Each ad was analyzed by typeface used in headlines, subheads, and copy. Each typeface received one point per use in headline, subhead, and copy. The sum of the points is the basis for the ranking.

Since not every ad contains headlines, subheads, and copy, there is no logical relationship between total points and the number of ads examined.

This is pitiful, and makes one wonder about the state of German creativity. Isn't it enough that after "streamlining," cars look more and more alike? It is more difficult to distinguish among them, and consequently more difficult for advertisers to develop ad campaigns for new models. We shouldn't, however, put on the brakes for the typography.

Put the pedal to the metal!

United States 1994

Type usage in 31 ads for 26 car brands

Type	Occurrence		
Garamond	●●●●● ●●●●● ●		
Goudy Old Style	●●●●● ●●●●●		
Caslon	●●●●● ●●		
Baskerville	●●●●●		
Franklin Gothic	●●●●●		
Futura	●●●●●		
Cochin	●●●●●		
Palatino	●●●●		
Weiß-Antiqua	●●●●	60%	
Bodoni	●●●	Mramor	●●
Cheltenham	●●●	Optima	●●
Corporate ASE	●●●	Adobe Trajan	●
Helvetica	●●●	ITC Avant Garde Gothic	●
ITC Weidemann	●●●	Bodoni Open	●
Bernhard Modern	●●	Century Old Style	●
ITC Galliard	●●	Grotesque No. 7	●
Gill Sans	●●	Kennerley	●
Matrix	●●	Volvo Script	●

In total, 87 occurrences, 27 different typefaces
60 % of the occurrences in 9 different typefaces

International brands and their typefaces

All of this can't be because of the frequently
cited conservative customer who sup-
posedly always wants to see the same typeface. Only two car manufacturers, Volkswagen and Mercedes, have used the same
typeface for several years. Neither Volkswagen nor Renault use their corporate
typefaces all the way into their print advertising. Volvo and Mercedes have exclusive
typefaces. In Europe, Alfa-Romeo, Opel,
and Saab have consistent type representa-
tion. Lexus, General Motors, Citroën,
and Peugeot use a different typeface for
almost every model. It's questionable
whether that is an especially good idea,
but it is definitely not a good idea to use
the same or a similar typefaces for similar
products of different brands.

**Put the pedal
to the metal**

Germany 1990 – 1992

Type usage in 31 ads for 29 car brands

Type	Occurrence		
Futura	●●●●● ●●●●● ●●●●● ●●●●● ●●		
Univers	●●●●● ●●●		
Bodoni	●●●●● ●●		
Franklin Gothic	●●●●● ●●		
Helvetica	●●●●● ●		
Times	●●●●● ●		**60%**

Gill Sans	●●●●	Bookman	●
ITC Kabel	●●●●	Caledonia	●
Arrow	●●●	Centaur	●
Optima	●●●	Impact	●
Century	●●	ITC Avant Garde Gothic	●
Corporate ASE	●●	ITC Berkeley Old Style	●
Diotima	●●	Janson	●
Madison	●●	Lectura	●
Walbaum	●●	Perpetua	●
Baskerville	●	Radiant	●
Bembo	●		

*In total, 92 occurrences, 27 different typefaces
60 % of the occurrences in 6 different typefaces*

Sieh da, es gibt noch andere Hersteller mit integrierten Kindersitzen.

Australisches Mandarinmodell Macropus rufus.

► 1692 strandete Francisco Pelsaert an der Küste Australiens und sah zum ersten Mal ein Modell mit integriertem Kindersitz. Als er davon zu Hause erzählte, tippte man sich nur an die Stirn.

► Über 300 Jahre später gilt der integrierte Kindersitz als eine der sinnvollsten Innovationen im Automobilbau. Wir haben diese Idee noch ein wenig verbessert: Zum ersten Mal gibt es ein Auto mit zwei integrierten Kindersitzen. Sehr zur Freude aller, die mehr als nur die durchschnittlichen 1,2 Kinder haben. Die besagten Sitze finden Sie auf Wunsch in der C-Klasse. Dem Auto, das auto motor sport zum sichersten seiner Klasse gekürt hat. Wir finden: ein guter Platz, um groß zu werden.

Mercedes-Benz
Ihr guter Stern auf allen Straßen.

Many designers are afraid that it will stifle their creativity if they use a type-face that is a predetermined corporate design. These ads prove the contrary. Mercedes-Benz can afford to forego pictures of cars and use children's drawings because the typesetting and typeface have already alerted the audience to what the ad is about.

Germany 1993 – 1995

Type usage in 31 ads for 29 car brands

Schrift	*Vorkommen*		
Futura	●●●●● ●●●●● ●●●●● ●		
Akzidenz Grotesk	●●●●● ●●		
Franklin Gothic	●●●●● ●●		
Garamond	●●●●● ●●		
Gill Sans	●●●●● ●		
Helvetica	●●●●● ●		
Bodoni	●●●●	**60%**	
Corporate ASE	●●●	Univers	●●
Optima	●●●	Bembo	●
Rotis	●●●	Caslon	●
Times	●●●	Centaur	●
Weiß-Antiqua	●●●	ITC Cheltenham	●
Arrow	●●	Handwriting	●
ITC Kabel	●●	ITC Korinna	●
Lucian	●●	Cochin	●
Rockwell	●●		

In total, 85 occurrences, 24 different typefaces
60 % of the occurrences in 7 different typefaces

Ein Auto darf nicht die Welt kosten.

► Wer sich in unserem Universum umschaut, merkt schnell, daß es für unsere Erde nirgendwo eine Reparaturwerkstatt oder Ersatzteile gibt. Alles, was wir mit dieser Erde anstellen, müssen wir selbst verantworten, selbst in Ordnung bringen oder selbst aushaden. Als Erfinder des Autos stehen wir natürlich ganz besonders in der Pflicht. Und wir wissen, daß wir diese Pflicht noch lange nicht erfüllt haben. Auch wenn z. B. unser E 300 DIESEL als erster und einziger die schärfsten Diesel-Abgasnormen der Welt (die von Kalifornien) erfüllt. ► Richtiger Umweltschutz wird bei uns bereits da umgesetzt, wo Autos entstehen – z. B. in unserem Werk in Rastatt. Und endet dort, wo sie verschwinden: beim Recycling. Wir wissen, für die Natur kann man nie genug tun. Aber wir arbeiten daran. Schließlich geht es auch um die Existenz des Autos.

Mercedes-Benz
Ihr guter Stern auf allen Straßen.

49

Great Britain 1990 – 1992
Type usage in 31 ads for 29 car brands

Type	*Occurrence*		
Futura	●●●●● ●●●●● ●●●●● ●●●●● ●●		
Helvetica	●●●●● ●●●●		
Franklin Gothic	●●●●●		
Baskerville	●●●●		
ITC Fenice	●●●●		
Bembo	●●●		
Bodoni	●●●		
Lucian	●●●		
Venus	●●●		
Augustea Neo	●●		
ITC Berkeley Old Style	●●		**60%**

Copperplate	●●	Clearface Gothic	●
Frutiger	●●	Corporate A·S·E	●
Gill Sans	●●	DIN 1451 Mittelschrift	●
Harry Obese	●●	Doric	●
Information	●●	Folio	●
Permanent Headline	●●	Grotesque No. 9b	●
Poppl Pontifex	●●	Jenson	●
Quadriga Antiqua	●●	News Gothic	●
Rockwell	●●	Newtext	●
Annonce	●	GST Polo	●
Arrow	●	Syntax	●
Bodoni Titling	●	Vendôme	●
Caslon	●	Volvo Script	●
Century	●	Weiß-Antiqua	●
Century Schoolbook	●		

*In total, 98 occurrences, 40 different typefaces
60 % of the occurrences in 11 different typefaces*

National markets and their typefaces

Nationalistic type markets still seem to
exist. In Great Britain, English-designed
typefaces such as Baskerville, Gill Sans,
and Rockwell are used more frequently
than German-designed faces; Futura is
used more often in Germany than in Great
Britain. This nationalistic tendency becomes even more pronounced when the
percentage of the German-designed Akzi-
denz Grotesk and Optima are calculated.
Goudy Old Style is typically used in the
United States, and new American typefaces,

Great Britain 1994
Type usage in 31 ads for 29 car brands

Type	Occurrence		
Futura	●●●●● ●●●●● ●		
Garamond	●●●●● ●●●●●		
Gill Sans	●●●●● ●		
Baskerville	●●●		
Helvetica	●●●		
Rockwell	●●●		
Akzidenz Grotesk	●●		
Albertus	●●		
Bembo	●●		
Bodoni	●●		
Corporate A·S·E	●●		
ITC Fenice	●●		**60%**
Folio	●●	ITC Cheltenham	●
Franklin Gothic	●●	Cloister	●
Frutiger	●●	Doric	●
Joanna	●●	Ehrhardt	●
Latin	●●	Fairfield	●
Life	●●	Fournier	●
Monkton	●●	Heathrow	●
Rotis	●●	Cochin	●
Times	●●	Lucian	●
Volvo Script	●●	Placard	●
ITC Berkeley	●	Vendôme	●
Century	●		

In total, 81 occurrences, 35 different typefaces
60 % of the occurrences in 12 different typefaces

such as Mramor and Matrix, are accepted more readily there than in Europe.

No dominant typeface for cars

Unlike cosmetics, there is no dominant typeface in the car industry. Although Futura is used frequently, it is not used significantly more than in other product groups. If Futura was the "right" typeface for this product group then similar typefaces such as ITC Avant Garde Gothic, would appear much more often. We should note that the popularity of sans serif typefaces decreases the further west you go.

Mediocrity is always the correct weight; except its scales are not true.

Anselm Feuerbach (1829 – 1880)
Philosopher, Germany

Avoiding mediocrity does not necessarily lead to extravagance. Look at the typefaces shown above, and compare the classically proportioned Univers with the top-heavy FF Balance: as in life, a small change in weight can make a difference in performance.

Type: Univers (upper lines)
and FF Balance (lower line)

**Advertising
monotony**

Ads in Stern *and* Spiegel *1992-1994*

Advertising monotony

Now that more typefaces than ever are being sold, fewer than ever are being used. This result of an AdFinder type analysis of *Stern* and *Spiegel* ads during the years 1992 to 1994, is, to be frank, pathetic – 551 ads from different industries were analyzed for typographic content in headlines, sub-heads, and copy. (*Stern* is a weekly magazine that covers popular culture and its icons in a slightly sensational way. *Spiegel* is also a weekly; it gives in-depth coverage of politics, the economy, and other more serious issues of the day.)

 stern DER SPIEGEL

The disturbing result

Forty-two typefaces were used in 1215 instances. But only 7 different typefaces were used for 69 percent of them, a total of 844 instances! Unbelievably, 523 occurrences (43 percent of the total) used 3 typefaces, namely Futura, Helvetica, and Garamond. Fourth through seventh places are held by Univers, Times, Bodoni, and Franklin Gothic.

Since 1992, this is what happened to the top seven: Top-ranked Futura took the lead again in 1994 after dropping to second place behind Helvetica in 1993. Garamond fell from second place in 1992 to fourth place in 1994. Even greater losses were felt by Times: still number 3 in 1992, plummeting to number 7 in 1994. Univers moved up from seventh place in 1992 to third place in 1994. The numbers of annually used typefaces stayed fairly constant at around 45, independent of the number of ads. It appears ad designers can't handle more than that.

All the ads were professionally designed by renowned agencies, not amateur desk-

Type Analysis of Ads in *Stern* and *Spiegel* 1992 – 1994

Type	1992	1993	1994	Type
Futura				Futura
Garamond				Helvetica
Helvetica				Univers
Times				Garamond
Bodoni				Bodoni
Franklin Gothic				Franklin Gothic
Univers				Times
Gill Sans				Century
ITC Avant Garde				Handwriting
Century				Gill Sans
Handwriting				Frutiger
Frutiger				ITC Avant Garde
Percentage of total number of occurrences	*77%*	*80%*	*72%*	
Total number of typefaces	*48*	*45*	*46*	

Based on Stern *and* Spiegel *issues Number 14 from the years 1992, 1993, and 1994, fewer than 50 different typefaces were used in advertisements per issue. Only 82 different typefaces were used for all the advertising, 75 percent of which were set in 12 typefaces. So 35 different typefaces were left for 25 percent of the instances.*

top publishers. Are art directors afraid of typography? Advertising strategists complain more and more about the loss of brand power. And brand identification and brand loyalty are more difficult to create than ten or twenty years ago. Don't be surprised when you are overlooked if you can't think of anything else to wear but a grey uniform when it's foggy.

Variatio delectat
Variety pleases

Proverb

Type: Caslon Antique

Fresh typefaces

Fresh typefaces

Campaign: Amstel; Product: Beer;
Country: The Netherlands; Type: Eden (modified)

Campaign: Drum; Product: Tobacco;
Country: The Netherlands; Type: Custom Design

New typefaces

If you are on the lookout for new typefaces, there is plenty of stimulation in the European print market; look especially at The Netherlands, Great Britain, Spain, and Italy, whose designers have given advertisements plenty of innovative and creative effort.

Netherlands

AMSTEL: For a real person a real beer with a real typeface.
DRUM: A typical example of non-design that cleverly takes the trends of the target audience and ricochets them right back. Working to address "young people" with a type design that looks squarely at the "self-

Campaign: Ariel; Product: Detergent;
Country: Great Britain; Type: FF Dolores

Campaign: MTV; Product: Music Television;
Country: Great Britain; Type: FF Trixie

made" product and trend, it comes with
an alternate touch that fits neatly into the
"self-made" total design.

Great Britain

ARIEL: *Finally,* different detergent advertising. Not only a picture with verve, but
a witty typeface supporting the overall
character of the ad.
MTV has proven itself a trendsetter by
using Carol Twombly's Lithos. MTV spon-
taneously adopts and spreads the newest
trends not only on the music scene, but
also with their use of special effects on
images and type.

RELIABLE
STRONG
YET
SENSITIVE

Campaign: Femidom; Product: Female Condoms;
Country: Great Britain; Type: Gill Sans (modified)

SABOR AMERICANO
POR UN DOLAR[*]

Campaign: Winns; Product: Cigarettes; Country: Spain;
Type: Industria

FEMIDOM: The English ad for female condoms is not only well written – "reliable
strong yet sensitive" – but is also typographically sincere. The headline typeface
(Gill Sans) was modified with wavy lines.

Spain

WINNS: The cigarette ad set in Industria
shows how the Spanish emulate the
American lifestyle. A touch of the Wild
West with Spanish elegance – that's it!

Campaign: Quorum; Product: Perfume;
Country: Spain; Type: OCR-B

Campaign: Once; Product: Fund-raising Lottery;
Country: Spain; Type: Custom Design

QUORUM: What does the Spanish man have in his pocket? A collection of very personal "necessities." Even ads can be equipped with typographic collector's items. Here is OCR-B – the once-maligned computer typeface, now trendy type Number 1 in Europe.

ONCE: A wonderfully antique, romantic type for moments worth remembering. The use of this typeface fully complements the advertising strategy. Once is a lottery that raises funds for the blind.

per maggior
sicurezza
allacciare
più di
una
cintura

Campaign: El Campero; Product: Fashion; Country: Italy; Type: Helvetica (antiqued)

Italy

EL CAMPERO: With a little imagination you can even make something original out of plain old Helvetica: This classic was antiqued for a belt ad. Successful type-recycling.

PHILIPPE MATIGNON: The headline is set in FF Beowulf. This random typeface really does behave like a werewolf with a constantly mutating face. Through clever Post-Script programming, each letter is different every time it's used (compare the n left and right).

Campaign: Matignon; Product: Fashion;
Country: Italy; Type: FF Beowolf

Campaign: BASF; Product: Compact Cassette;
Country: Germany; Types: FF Trixie, FF Mambo,
FF Harlem, F Lushus

Germany

BASF: The typography of German industrial companies usually appears conservative, serious, and severe – if not actually boring. This example shows that it can be different! Four brand new typefaces for headlines in one ad add up to typographic fireworks that will strike with teutonic precision right into the hearts of the target group.

The chains of habit
are too light,
so one would feel them
before they are too tight
to still throw them off.

Samuel Johnson (1709 – 1784)
Lexicographer, Critic, Conversationalist,
Great Britain

Type: ITC Berkeley Old Style

**American
quartet**

*Campaign: Motorola: Product: Computer-Board;
Type: ITC Berkeley Old Style; Country: United States*

The four most popular typefaces in the United States

It seems every hemisphere has its own type preferences. While in Germany the Futura, Helvetica, Garamond, Times quartet represents a large part of the printed advertising market, in the United States the cards are shuffled differently: ITC Garamond, Palatino, ITC Berkeley Old Style, and Bernhard Modern.

The most frequently seen typeface in the United States is ITC Garamond, which is comparable in use to Times in Germany. ITC Garamond is enormously popular because it was one of the first digital Garamonds available, and because its large

*Campaign: Aussie; Product: Shampoo;
Type: ITC Garamond; Country: United States*

*Campaign: Hanes; Product: Stockings;
Type: Garamond; Country: United States*

Garamond Adobe

Garamond Berthold

Garamond Stempel

&

Garamond ITC

Garamond Linotype No. 3

Garamond Simoncini

x-height allows for high legibility. The fact that it is not a "true" Garamond has given it a bad reputation among some typographers.

Palatino is also very popular in the United States, especially for pure image advertising: computers, cosmetics, and business. The world of finance and business seems to have a special fondness for ITC Berkeley Old Style. Bernhard Modern is preferred for fashion, cosmetics, and food.

A fitting anecdote: When the new Rotis was released in 1988 in Paris, the official typeface for the Olympic Games in Barce-

There are many Garamonds. On top, three "real" ones, on the bottom three "fake" ones. The fake Garamonds apparently all originated with type specimens mistakenly attributed at the beginning of this century to the punch-cutter Claude Garamond. The error was dis-covered as early as 1926, but since these false Garamonds were already generating good sales, the mistake was never corrected.

"Who's going to make sure the trees will be here tomorrow?"

"Not an easy question. But that's what my son asked the other day. He's

thinking about it. Just like everybody. He wants to know if the trees will still

be around when he grows up. Well, working for Georgia-Pacific like I do, I

can tell him we're doing our part. Planting new trees by the millions.

Setting aside land. Making sure the trees will always be here. For everybody.

Of course, I can't speak for other companies out there. But I know we're

doing what's right." Steve Delfs, Forester. **Georgia-Pacific** ◬

Campaign: Georgia-Pacific; Product: Finance;
Country: United States; Type: Bernhard Modern

lona was announced at the same event. The officials proclaimed with a grand gesture that it was decided that the "famous typefaces" Times and Helvetica would be used for the Olympics instead of a design that had already been specially commissioned. Roaring laughter in the audience.

It is not known if anyone laughed when the announcement was made that ITC Garamond was selected as the official typeface for the 1996 Olympic Games in Atlanta, Georgia.

To keep your business on the move, send it our way.

Above: *Campaign: Greater Phoenix; Product: Image; Country: USA; Type: Palatino*

Greater Phoenix, growing in the right direction.

Below: *Campaign: Lark; Product: Suitcases; Country: USA; Type: Bernhard Modern*

The easy way to handle success.

Hamburgefonts
Hamburgefonts
Hamburgefonts
Hamburgefonts
Bernhard Modern

Hamburgefonts
Hamburgefonts
Lucian

Hamburgefonts
Hamburgefonts
Hamburgefonts
Hamburgefonts
Cochin

Hamburgefonts
Hamburgefonts
Nicolas Cochin

Several other typefaces also ride the wave of success of the graceful Bernhard Modern. One is Lucian, from the same designer, and the French Cochins. At first glance they look very similar. Looking closer,

especially at the italics, only the large capital letters and the long ascenders are a common feature. There aren't quite as many "Cochins" as "Garamonds" but the differences are greater among them.

IT IS NOT THE CAPITAL
THAT CONNECTS US
BUT THE SMALL CAP.

Hans Peter Willberg
Typographer, teacher, Germany

Hans Peter Willberg is one of the leading
German typography evangelists and
is the author on several books on type
and typography.

Type: Latienne

**Capitals and
small caps**

FOR ALL THOSE
WAITING FOR THE
PERFECT BALANCE OF
HAND CRAFTSMANSHIP,
ADVANCED TECHNOLOGY,
AND A LOOK THAT'LL
KNOCK THE WIND
RIGHT OUT OF YOU…

Fake small caps: Advanced technology?
Typeface: Goudy Old Style

*Why you can't capitalize on unreal
small caps*

Small caps are noble, reliable, confidence
inspiring. So it's no surprise that banks
and credit institutions, purveyors of high-
yield investments and consumable products, and high-tech service companies
frequently display their "capital" messages
this way. This trend is especially apparent in
the United States. In principle, there is
nothing to be said against it except that
legibility suffers in longer headlines.

FOR ALL THOSE WAITING FOR THE PERFECT BALANCE OF HAND CRAFTMANSHIP, ADVANCED TECHNOLOGY, AND A LOOK THAT'LL KNOCK THE WIND RIGHT OUT OF YOU...

The perfect balance: Real small caps
Typeface: Goudy Catalogue

German typography professor and designer Hans Peter Willberg once said in conversation with fellow typographers: "It is not the capital that connects us but the small cap."

Capitals and small caps

That a mysterious connection between the capital and small caps does exist is neatly shown in the Schwab ad. American bankers apparently have a preference for letting the small capitals work for them-

OUR BUSINESS SERVICES ARE DESIGNED TO IMPROVE YOUR STANDING NOT JUST WITH THE CEO, BUT ALSO WITH THE CFO.

selves. But it is not as simple as it seems: Real small caps are different from computer-compressed capitals, which look like they were washed in water that was too hot. If they are also spaced too closely, as in the Schwab ad, a very negative message appears "between the lines."

The perfect balance between craftsmanship and technology is certainly not appar-

THE JAPANESE DIET TO GET FAT OVERSEAS.

ent in the typography in the ad on the previous page. Before long the opposite is conveyed because small caps are just as problematic in text as caps. With several lines of text, it hampers reading and makes comprehension more difficult.

If someone loses twenty pounds, then his or her figure will have different proportions. It's not any different when small caps are made out of caps – not even after a Japanese diet – even if it looks that way here.

Real small caps have been designed by type designers so that a smooth and har-

74

monious type picture is portrayed. This involves line weight, spacing, and several other characteristics. Today many digitized typefaces include real small caps. They can be found as Small Cap Fonts, in Expert Sets, and they are easy as pie to access.

POOR OLD MOUSE.

Typeface: Futura

Saving money by not investing in real small caps will result in messages that carry the wrong signals. Who here is the least well off? The advertiser who can't afford real small caps, the tortured type – or the audience?

With fake small caps the first letters appear blown up, clumsy, and awkward. They are also glued too closely to the second let-

CAREFREE® INTRODUCES THE FIRST PANTILINER WITH DOUBLE BARRIER PROTECTION.

Typeface: Seneca

ter and suffocate the rest of the type with their excess weight. Instead of rolling hills, there are big mountains in front of each word! You instantly lose interest in reading and the information is lost.

Most imitators are drawn
to the inimitable.

Marie von Ebner-Eschenbach (1830 – 1916)
Novelist, poet, Austria

Type: Apple Garamond

Pears into apples …

Pears into apples …

Campaign: Intel; Product: Microprocessors;
Type: ITC Garamond; Country: United States

How type copiers make Apple stronger

Remember the 1960s? The duck tail was a must for every fan who wanted to imitate Elvis. Even today teens around the world try to grab a little glitter by copying the clothes and mannerisms of their stars and idols. Happily this stops after young people mature and find their own identity. In the long run it would be pretty boring with thousands of Elvis clones.

All told, the only one to profit from all the copying was Elvis. His fame grew proportionally to the number of imitators – just the way any star, brand, or identity is strengthened, not weakened, by imitators.

Campaign: Apple; Product: Computers;
Type: ITC Garamond; Country: Germany

From this point of view, the results of our examination of advertising in the computer industry gives plenty to think about. Over fifty computer manufacturers are zealously strengthening Apple by copying its typographic appearance. All use ITC Garamond.

What happens when pears want to be apples? The world will begin to think that pears are second-class and that apples are the only thing worth having. The computer companies listed here suggest, unintentionally, the same thing with their imitated type: Apple is the only real computer.

Campaign: NEC; Product: Laserprinters;
Type: ITC Garamond; Country: Germany

One appears in the guise of the trendsetter
with the hope that Apple's image and success will rub off on its product, implying
that their product is not strong enough to
have its own identity.

Perhaps it's because the computer industry is relatively young. These copycat companies shouldn't, however, give themselves
too much more time to find an identity.
Otherwise, interest in their products will
be short-lived.

Type Analysis ITC Garamond

Industry: computers; Years: 1988 – 1994

Brand	Country	Brand	Country
Aladdin	USA	NEC	Austria
Amstrad	France	NEC	Germany
Analog Devices	USA	NEC	France
Brother	USA	NEC	USA
Cadkey	USA	Optronics	USA
CH Products	USA	Osborne	USA
Cobra	USA	Panasonic	Germany
Compaq	Austria	Panasonic	USA
Compaq	Germany	Paoku	Germany
Easyreader	Great Britain	Pioneer	Austria
Eizo	Austria	Pixelworks	USA
Encad	USA	Princeton	USA
Epson	Austria	Quantum	USA
Epson	Germany	RIO	Italy
Fifth Generation	USA	Sharp	USA
Grafpoint	USA	Sony	USA
Harris	USA	Summagraphics	USA
Howtek	USA	Teknigraphics	USA
Intel	USA	Texas Instruments	Germany
Intergraph	USA	Toshiba	Germany
Letraset	Germany	Toshiba	Great Britain
Maqni	USA	Truevision	USA
Media Cybernetics	USA	Vermont	USA
Mitac	USA	View Sonic	USA
National Semicond.	USA	Wacom	USA

The sad result:
43 brands used ITC Garamond in at least 50 campaigns from 1988 to 1994 .

Pears into apples …

ITC Garamond light
ITC Garamond light, 80%
Apple Garamond light
ITC Garamond light cond.

ITC *Garamond* light italic
ITC *Garamond* light italic, 80%
Apple *Garamond* light italic
ITC *Garamond* light cond. italic

ITC **Garamond** bold
ITC **Garamond** bold, 80%
Apple **Garamond** bold
ITC **Garamond** bold cond.

ITC ***Garamond*** bold italic
ITC ***Garamond*** bold italic, 80%
Apple ***Garamond*** bold italic
ITC ***Garamond*** bold cond. italic

Even ITC Garamond is not what it used to be – at least not for those who want to imitate Apple's typographic appearance. At first glance what appears to be ITC Garamond condensed is actually something quite different.

In 1990 Apple contracted Bitstream to redesign ITC Garamond. "Apple Garamond" has existed ever since. It is very much like ITC Garamond except narrower by 80 percent and a little heavier. Distinct differences are evident in the light and bold italics.

I consider myself
a seducer
and seducing people
is sweaty work.

Werner Herrwerth
Advertiser, journalist, publisher, Germany

*Werner Herrwerth worked in the advertising
trade for over forty-five years. He owned
five agencies in Munich, and was involved
in the marketing of 75 brand names and
1200 ad campaigns. He is now working as
a publisher, and still runs an ad agency,
Senior Marketing.*

Type: Berthold Signata

**Mask of
the cosmetic
industry**

Mask of the cosmetic industry

ALMAY

GUINOT

ENERGANCE

VITAL-PERFECTION

COVER GIRL

POND'S

PLÉNITUDE

HR

EFFIDOSE FUCUS

PAYOT

SATINA

UP LIFT

Optima – the optima(l) typeface?

Recent studies of several international cosmetics ads show that Optima is used almost without exception. And that worldwide! This is so phenomenal that you don't really know whether to laugh or cry about it.

You could laugh because obviously users and clients have accepted as fact that it actually does matter what type is used, and that certain typefaces fit only specific product groups. Otherwise we would find the standard mix of Helvetica, Futura, Times, or Courier in cosmetics advertising. But this is not the case.

84

**Mask of
the cosmetic
industry**

ESTĒE LAUDER

CLINIQUE

ʃHIʃEIDO

FRENCHTOP®

BIGUINE

CRISTAL MECHES

GUERLAIN

GATINEAU

Silvikrin

OENOBIOL

You could cry because the cosmetics industry is clinging like a drowning person to a piece of driftwood – in this case Optima – even though shiploads of other typefaces are floating around nearby.

Since the entire industry relies on this one typeface, it is very difficult for the consumer to find a brand in this product group that is different from the others. Where is the product that will make the consumer feel special? Whether it's "pure energy" or "natural radiance," "unique vitamin complex," or "beauty sense" – everything hides behind the same mask.

Headache or boredom …

In the formidable search for an original
brand personality, the consumer could get
a headache, or fall asleep from boredom.
One might even get the idea that all those
bottles and tubes contain the same thing.

Alternatives

Whoever wants to play it safe can choose
a typeface similar to Optima, for example,
Peignot. But since it is slightly formal,
Peignot should be used only for a logotype.
You could then look at typefaces with a
similar style or rhythm as Optima: There
are a few alternatives on page 87 worth
considering.

…until you fall asleep? No wonder with so much Optima!

Hamburgefonts
Hamburgefonts
Optima

Hamburgefonts
Hamburgefonts
Signata

Hamburgefonts
Hamburgefonts
Poppl Laudatio

Hamburgefonts
Hamburgefonts
Today Sans Serif

Hamburgefonts
Hamburgefonts
Formata

Hamburgefonts
ITC Eras

HAMBURGEFONTS
Lithos

*On the left, some alternatives to Optima;
on the right our suggestions for those who really
want to set themselves apart.*

The secret of type
is that it speaks

Paul Claudel (1868 – 1955)
Poet and statesman, France

Type: Creme

**Five letters
conquer
the world**

Nivea – the elite of brand typography

What is a brand? According to Hans
Domizlaff, a prominent brand and identity
expert, there is no such thing. It is a void,
a phantom existing as a live and soulful
being only in the minds of consumers. How
do you get such a phantom to inhabit
the consciousness? With type! A brand that
has done it like no other is Nivea. You can
almost smell the Nivea scent just by looking at their typefaces.

Nivea Bold was developed by Günther
Heinrich at the TBWA advertising agency in
Hamburg in 1992 from the original logo-
type, which was created in the 1930s.
Heinrich used it as the model for Nivea
Bold typeface.

Through an international image campaign Nivea
prepared the market for widespread marketing
of the creme to all areas of the cosmetics industry.
With urgency and at the same time, subtlety, the
new type (based on the original Nivea logo) conveys

that something sensational has been happening
with the brand. Such a strategy was possible only
because the Nivea logo has been imprinted in
people's minds for decades, therefore, even the
smallest change is perceived as sensational.

First of all, he had to visualize the consistent corporate presentation of a brand whose product philosophy is "pure & simple". Nivea Bold became the permanent headline typeface for worldwide advertising. Creme type, designed in the United States, was added as a complement. Heinrich: "The communication center of the Nivea umbrella brand is the creme. Its formal identity is defined by the harmonious order of opposites. For that the Creme type is necessary."

Nivea as an umbrella brand for cosmetic products has a worldwide market share of 35 percent – a success only dreamed of by other brands.

Five letters conquer the world

ABCD EFGH IJKL MNOP QRS TUVW XYZ

ABCD EFGH IJKL MNOP QRS TUVW XYZ

Metroblack (left) was the design inspiration for the 1930s Nivea logo (below). In 1992 the new Nivea Bold alphabet (right) was modeled on the original five letters by Gisela Will of EF Fontinform in Hamburg under the direction of Günther Heinrich of the TBWA agency.

This phenomenon has occurred even though Nivea advertising denies following current trends and advertising techniques. Next to Nivea, only the elite of strong brand personalities, for example, IBM, Marlboro, and Mercedes, can afford to be this casual. Common characteristic of these four top brands: they have used the same typographic image for several years, they take care that no exceptions appear, and their typography is recognized internationally.

*Kathy Schinhoven developed the typeface
Creme to complement Nivea Bold.*

A word resembles
a bee: it has honey,
and a sting.

Talmud

Type: ITC Novarese

**The real
and the fake**

I don't see the point of getting engaged
I don't see the point of getting
I don't see the point of
I don't see the point
I don't see the
I don't see
I don't
I do

Campaign: De Beers; Product: Diamonds;
Country: Great Britain; Type: Augustea Nova

Diamond campaign under the glass

Type has to relate to the product so the
subconscious can be "programmed."
Ideally, the typography mirrors the product's qualities and steers audience attention
in the right direction before one word is
read. The English diamond campaign is an
especially well-done example of this.

This ad was well thought out from the
initial concept to the final dot. Augustea
Nova was chosen to carry it off. Its serifs,
apostrophes, and i dots have sharp, bril-
liant contours – every letter polished like a
real diamond.

Für uns war es nicht immer leicht.

Für uns war es nicht immer

Für uns war es nicht

Für uns war es

Für uns war

Für uns ist

Für Dich

Ein Diamant ist unvergänglich.

*Campaign: De Beers; Product: Diamonds;
Country: Germany; Type: ITC Novarese*

There was more than the problem of keeping the ambiguity in the copy in the translation into German. Unfortunately, the type selection was not as sensitive either, even though both the English and German typefaces were designed by Aldo Novarese, the highly praised Italian type designer. And the diamond was the victim! i dots became round and boring, the t lost its interesting facet on the cross bar, and the feet of the t and e were worn blunt on the road from England to Germany. Too bad, these aren't real diamonds anymore.

TELL ME THE PAST
AND I WILL RECOGNIZE
THE FUTURE.

Confucius (511 – 479 BC)
Philosopher, China

Carol Twombly's Lithos is inspired by ancient
Greek letterforms. Its tremendous success in the
marketplace was a complete surprise to everyone in the type trade.

Type: Lithos

**More than
blue smoke**

1959   1970

1981   1990

*Peter Stuyvesant – a brand through
changing times*

Type is not just blue smoke – it mirrors
the current culture, and can be an icon for
trends, developments, and idols. This is
plain as day in Peter Stuyvesant's advertising from the years 1959 to 1995. While the
logotype remained unchanged, the typography shows the spirit of the times in the
headlines and subheads.

In 1959 a modern, widely spaced sans
serif, Gill Sans, was used to show that whoever identified with the brand was open,
worldly, and widely traveled.

In the 1970s the slogan "the scent of the
big, wide world" becomes a person-to-

More than blue smoke

Die EG-Gesundheitsminister: Rauchen gefährdet die Gesundheit. Der Rauch einer Zigarette dieser Marke enthält 0,8 mg Nikotin und 12 mg Kondensat (Teer). (Durchschnittswerte nach ISO.)

Die EG-Gesundheitsminister: Rauchen gefährdet die Gesundheit. Der Rauch einer Zigarette dieser Marke enthält 0,8 mg Nikotin und 12 mg Kondensat (Teer). (Durchschnittswerte nach ISO.)

1994   1995

Type Analysis Peter Stuyvesant

Type	Year	Type	Year	Type	Year
Gill	1959	Futura	1972	Futura	1985
Gill	1960	Futura	1973	Futura	1986
Gill	1961	Futura	1974	Futura	1987
Volta	1962	Futura	1975	Arsis	1988
Bodoni	1963	Futura	1976	Handwriting	1989
Univers	1964	Futura	1977	Handwriting	1990
Times	1965	Futura	1978	Futura	1991
Times	1966	Futura	1979	Handwriting	1992
Times	1967	Futura	1980	Handwriting	1993
Volta	1968	Futura	1981	Handwriting	1994
Univers	1969	Beton	1982	Handwriting	1995
Clearface	1970	Beton	1983		
Futura	1971	Beton	1984		

person connection with closely set Clearface and its comfortable, softly rounded edges.

The unchecked growth of the 1980s shows itself in the dramatically inclined narrow bold Futura (then still something special).

The ads from the 1990s mirror the change to a less complicated, more personal lifestyle with handwriting – continuing with the campaign "Come together."

What do you think would have happened if Peter Stuyvesant had set everything in Times or Helvetica?

There is nothing
more important
in the world
than enticing people
to think.

Sigmund Graff (1898 – 1979)
Writer, Germany

Type: Find out in the next chapter!

**Are you
type conscious?**

Type: Century Schoolbook

Type: Univers

Type: ITC Fenice

Type: Bodoni

Test it now!

After reading this book, have you turned into a type with more awareness, or could you still possibly be a type heathen? You can find out here in three steps.

FIRST STEP: Look at the sixteen ads from the French department store chain "Monoprix" on pages 104 to 107. The prize-winning campaign shows a colorful spectrum of different typefaces. What's the first thing that comes to mind?

Type: Bernhard Modern

Type: Permanent Headline

Type: Futura

Type: Times

SECOND STEP: Compare your personal impressions with the opinions in the box on page 106, and assess them by circling the letters in the columns "perfectly true," "sort-of true," "absolutely false."

THIRD STEP: Count how many times you circled the letters P, G or T.

Then find out on page 107 what kind of a type type you are.

Are you type conscious?

Type: Goudy Old Style

Type: Balladeer

Type: ITC Garamond

Type: Univers

Test your type awareness ...	perfectly true	sort of true	absolutely false
• Chaotic, those French	P	P	T
• It looks like lots of specialty stores under one roof	T	G	P
• What's with the type salad?	P	G	T
• They go to a lot of trouble for their clients	T	G	P
• Looks like a graphic designer wanted to show off	P	P	T
• These people have imagination	T	G	P
• I think this is overdone	P	G	T
• It must be fun to shop there	T	G	P
• I would love to do a campaign like this some time	T	T	P

**Are you
type conscious?**

Type: ITC Garamond

Type: Bernhard Modern

Type: Baskerville

Type: ITC Novarese

Evaluation

Count how many times you circled the letters
P, G, or T.

Mostly P
You have very plain type consciousness.
You'd better read the book again!

Mostly G
Your type consciousness still has grey areas.
Do something about it.

Mostly T
You really are a type-conscious type. High fives!

What I see
is not what I want!

Jelle Bosma
Typographer, Netherlands

Jelle Bosma is one of the few experts
devoted to finding a reasonable balance
between type design and font technology.
He has worked for Scangraphic, and since
1991, for Monotype Typography.

Type: Futura

If you want
to get what you
see ...

**If you want
to get what you
see ...**

The phrase "What you see is what you get" (WYSIWIG) has almost become the desktop publishing mantra. Unfortunately, it doesn't always coincide with reality, and when it comes to ordering type, the exact opposite is true. You have to look very carefully in the beginning to get what you want in the end.

THE QUICK BROWN FOX JUMPS OVER THE LAZY DOG

The quick brown fox jumps over the lazy dog

1234567890

The Linotype-Hell version of Futura LH Light. The spacing is open, and it's distinctly recognizable by the stronger stroke weights, the capital J, and the lining figures. The relationship between capital height and ascenders is more harmonious.

Linotype-Hell has good guidelines for ordering type: Do not order a typeface before you've seen the entire alphabet. In a detailed type catalog you can check if the recommended font is suitable for you. Are all weights available? Does it have the necessary accents? How does the type look in a range of sizes? Caution: Different manufacturers offer the same typefaces – there are definite differences in design and quality that are apparent only after close scrutiny.

Don't let the cat out of the bag

A good example of this problem is Futura designed by Paul Renner. It is a bestseller and there are many PostScript versions available. For example, one version has been reworked for better legibility for copy set in small sizes, another specifically for setting headline type for posters. It is fre-

**If you want
to get what you
see ...**

THE QUICK BROWN FOX JUMPS OVER THE LAZY DOG

The quick brown fox jumps over the lazy dog

1234567890

Futura Light, sold by Linotype and Adobe, is more suited for display work. Distinctly recognizable by the finer stroke weight and the stronger contrast between capital height and ascenders, this font is too light to be a text typeface.

quently recommended not to use the same type in the complete range of sizes. This is why some manufacturers offer different versions of the same font.

There are also many companies saturating the market with pirated typefaces. These typefaces usually have names similar to the original. But after a careful look, the differences quickly become evident. Not infrequently the accented characters, for instance the German umlauts (ä, ö, and ü), and other special signs are missing. Also, accents are incorrectly positioned above the letters.

**If you want
to get what you
see ...**

It is far safer to stick to quality fonts from well-known type manufacturers.

PostScript and TrueType

Digital type is offered in different data formats. The usual type formats for desktop publishers and professional users are PostScript Type1 and TrueType. Most professional studios work with PostScript because it has the best track record.

For PostScript typefaces, Adobe Type Manager, an additional piece of software, is necessary for the screen display. This automatically ensures the best possible showing

ZWÖLF SÜSSE BOXKÄMPFER

JAGTEN EVA QUER DURCH DAS IJSSELMEER

1234567890

The original typeface Arcadia (Linotype-Hell) contains all its characters and accents in perfect order.

of the type on screen. Extra software is not necessary for the TrueType format since it is already supported by system software (Apple Macintosh as of system 7.0 and Microsoft Windows as of version 3.1). TrueType fonts are user friendly.

TrueType fonts have recently been tested with good output results on high-resolution printers. Previously there were problems with TrueType fonts in service bureaus, mostly because printer drivers were not capable of handling the new format, and because of the inferior quality of pirated fonts.

Most fonts available today, both Post-Script and TrueType, work on Macintosh computers as well as PCs with Windows.

**If you want
to get what you
see ...**

Delivery Form

Fonts are usually delivered on diskette and include all weights in the type family. Some type sellers offer special delivery services, and will also create custom type packages for the client.

CD-ROMS are increasingly becoming the most popular form of font distribution. For a small basic fee a, CD-ROM encoded with all the typefaces in that manufactu-

ZU LF S SSE BOXK ÑPFER
JÄGTEN EVA QUER DURCH DAS IJSSELMEER
1234567890

Pirated type with uneven shapes. The most noticeable defects: the accented characters are missing, the G is too small on the bottom, the figures appear too bold, the spacing between the I and J is bad, and the space between words is obviously too large.

rer's library is mailed to the user. When ready to use a font, the user calls one of the unlocking centers, makes arrangements for payment, and is given the code to unlock the requested font.

Of course, there are also completely open type libraries on CD-ROM. This is a rather large investment, but for professionals who use many typefaces, and need to access them without delay, it is a good one. Delivery of fonts online is also offered, but at this time is not widely used. However, it probably won't be long before it's the preferred delivery method.

Ten commandments

**Do not pirate,
do not copy,
do not imitate**

Source: FontShop

You shall use only original typefaces.

You shall respect digital typefaces
as licensed software protected by law.

You shall not think
that as the buyer of a type package
you become its owner.
You only buy the usage rights.

You are only allowed
to print on one printer
with your type package:
the purchase does not entitle you to more.

You have to acquire a multi-printer license
if you want to print
on more than one printer.

for digital type users

**Do not pirate,
do not copy,
do not imitate**

You have to buy a multi-site license
if you want to use a font
in several locations
or offices of your company.

You shall not put your type
with your jobs for the service bureau.
A single license forbids this.

You may not copy fonts
without authorization: it is illegal!
The license rules only allow
a copy for back-up purposes.

You shall not use illegal type copies.
It damages the type designers
and inhibits the development
of new typefaces.

You shall immediately destroy
any illegal copies
that might be on your company network.
This is punishable by law.

Bibliography

Charles Bigelow, Paul Hayden Duensing, Linnea Gentry
Fine Print On Type

Lewis Blackwell
Twentieth Century Type

Alastair Campbell
The MacDesigner's Handbook

Sebastian Carter
Twentieth Century
Type Designers

Graphis Press Corp.
Graphis Typography 1

Jost Hochuli
Detail in Typography
Designing Books
Jost Hochuli's Alphabugs

Peter Karow
Font Technology –
Description and Tools

Alexandert Lawson
Anatomy of Typefaces

Robert Norton
Types Best Remembered /
Types Best Forgotten

Mac McGrew
American Metal Typefaces
of the twentieth Century

Ruari McLean
The Thames and Hudson Manual
of Typography
Jan Tschichold: Typographer
Typographers on Type

David Ogilvy
Ogilvy on Advertising

Christopher Perfect, Gordon Rookledge
Rookledge's International
Typefinder

Rick Poynor
Typography Now
The Graphic Edge

Herbert Spencer
Pioneers of Modern Typography

Erik Spiekermann
Rhyme & Reason:
A typographic novel

Erik Spiekermann & E. M. Ginger
Stop Stealing Sheep
& find out how type works

Sumner Stone
Typography on the Personal
Computer

James Sutton, Alan Bertram
An Atlas of Typeforms

Walter Tracy
Letters of Credit

Lawrence W. Wallis
Modern Encyclopedia
of Typefaces 1960 – 1990

Jon Wozencroft
The Graphic Language
of Neville Brody

About the authors

Stefan Rögener was the first to operate a photo-
typesetting studio in Hamburg, Germany. He is
a type consultant, and runs Germany's largest
ad library, AdFinder GmbH. He is the publisher
of the award-winning typography magazine
Satzspiegel; his co-authors, Ursula Packhäuser
and Albert-Jan Pool, are a writer/editor and the
designer, respectively.

Ursula Packhäuser studied music as a child,
and English and education at the University of
Hamburg. She worked in the classical department of RCA Records and was a product manager for Polygram Records. In 1983 she joined
the Haase companies group, where she is in
charge of advertising and public relations. Her
piano compositions were published in 1992.
She works as a freelance writer, and runs her
own advertising agency in Hamburg.

Albert-Jan Pool studied graphic design at
the Royal Academy of Arts, The Netherlands
where Gerrit Noordzij, professor of type design,
converted him to typography. The academic
was followed by the practical at the type studio
of Scangraphic. In 1991 he became artistic
director of the type department at URW. He has
designed several typefaces for URW and Font-
Shop. He works at his own studio, Dutch Design,
and teaches type design in Hamburg and Kiel.

*The authors would like to express their
special thanks to:*

*Frank Blokland of Dutch Type Library
Sabine Cara of Scangraphic PrePress Technology
Burwell Davis of Adobe Europe
Veronica Elsner and Günther Flake
of EF Fontinform
Ottmar Hoefer of Linotype-Hell
Bernd Möllenstädt of H. Berthold Systeme
Peter Rosenfeld of URW++
Jürgen Siebert of FontShop*

for supplying the fonts used in this book.

Editor
Stefan Rögener

Translation editor
E. M. Ginger

Concept and content
Karl-Ernst Gaertner
Ursula Packhäuser
Albert-Jan Pool
Stefan Rögener

Text
Ursula Packhäuser

English translation
Stephanie Tripier

Design and production
Albert-Jan Pool, Dutch Design

Cover design
Jeff Zwerner

Images
Marc Rögener

Film output
FaberPublish, Hamburg

Printer
Shepard Poorman, Indianapolis

Typefaces
Minion™
Design: Robert Slimbach, 1990
Adobe Systems Inc.
Myriad™ Multiple Master
Design: Robert Slimbach, Carol Twombly, 1992
Adobe Systems Inc.

Paper
St. Lawrence Cream Matte

Adobe Press books examine the art and
technology of digital communications.
Published by Macmillan Computer
Publishing, Adobe Press books can be
found wherever books about computers
and the communication arts are sold.